Curious Cat

Written by Andrea Butler
Illustrated by Mercedes McDonald

 ScottForesman

A Division of HarperCollins*Publishers*

2

Dad opened the car door.
In climbed Curious Cat.

Purr, purr, . . . silence.
Who needs a mat?

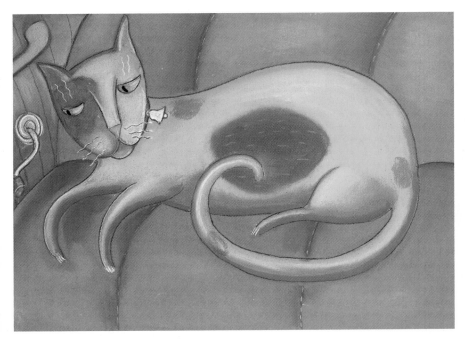

Dad opened the shopping bag.
In climbed Curious Cat.

Purr, purr, . . . silence.
Who needs a mat?

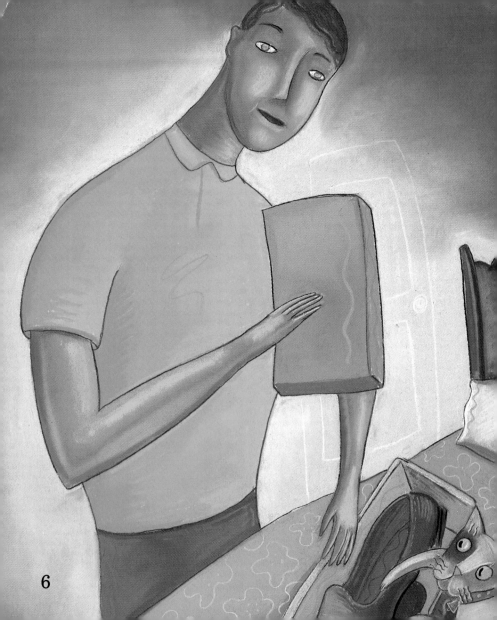

6

Dad opened the shoe box.
In climbed Curious Cat.

Purr, purr, . . . silence.
Who needs a mat?

Dad opened the closet.
In climbed Curious Cat.

Purr, purr, . . . silence.
Who needs a mat?

10

Dad opened the laundry bin.
In climbed Curious Cat.

Purr, purr, . . . silence.
Who needs a mat?

Dad opened the washing machine.
In climbed Curious Cat.

Purr, purr. . .

MEOW!!

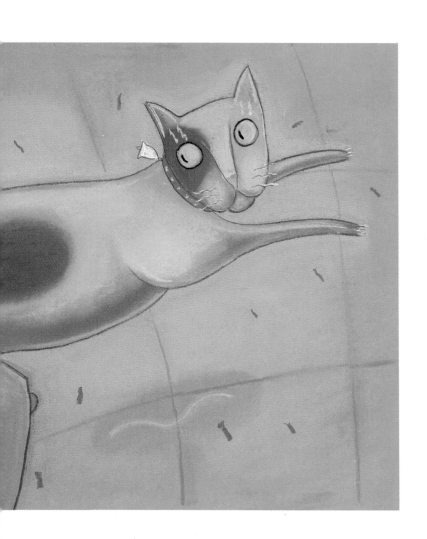

Who needs a mat?